Jazz Piano Trios

Conceived, Arranged, & Produced by Jim Odrich

ISBN 978-1-59615-091-1

Music Minus One

EXCLUSIVELY DISTRIBUTED BY

HAL•LEONARD®

Contact us:
Hal Leonard
7777 West Bluemound Road
Milwaukee, WI 53213
Email: info@halleonard.com

In Europe, contact:
Hal Leonard Europe Limited
42 Wigmore Street
Marylebone, London, W1U 2RN
Email: info@halleonardeurope.com

In Australia, contact:
Hal Leonard Australia Pty. Ltd.
4 Lentara Court
Cheltenham, Victoria, 3192 Australia
Email: info@halleonard.com.au

Jazz Piano Trios

Contents

Jim Odrich has enjoyed a varied experience in music as pianist, composer, and arranger. Although the great bulk of his work has been in the so-called jazz/pop category (for want of a better designation), his basic grounding has been in the so-called "classical" arena. He holds a master's degree in music, as well as a doctorate from Columbia University. His understanding of music is derived from solid, continuing study of the gamut of styles form Bach to all the present contemporary styles. Before entering the New York City music scene, he was a pianist-arranger of the famous "Airmen of Note" in Washington, D.C. along with close friends such as Sammy Nestico, Tommy Newsom, and Walt Levinsky. While there, he also wrote several arrangements for the USAF Symphony Orchestra. His familiarity with the construction and structure of what is generally referred to as "serious music" has permeated his compositions and is even apparent in his approach to jazz improvisation. He has composed and conducted music for symphony orchestra, national radio and television commercials, recordings, and has written several original serious piano compositions.

BUT BEAUTIFUL

Written by Johnny Burke & Jimmy Van Heusen

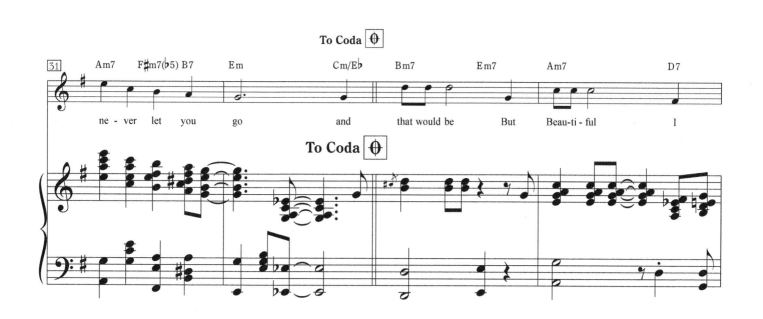

know

9

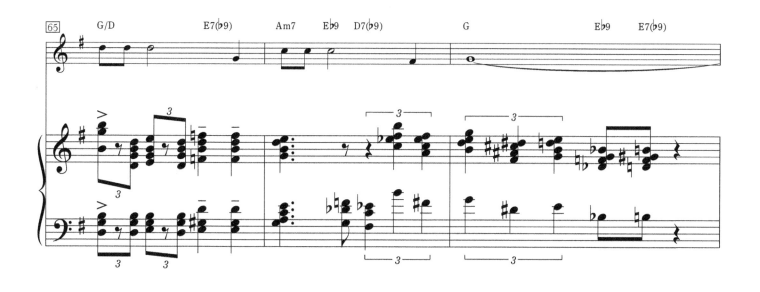

I'M GETTING SENTIMENTAL OVER YOU

Written by George Bassman & Ned Washington

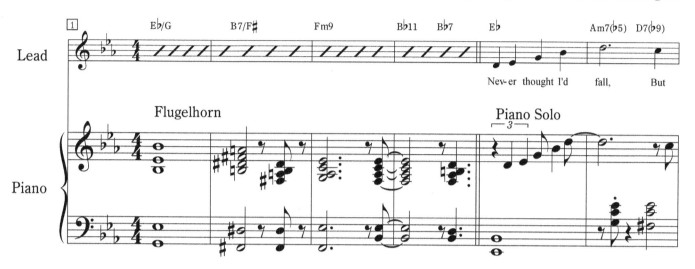

MMO 6009

through I'm Get- ting Sen - ti - men- tal Ov - er You

I thought I was hap - py, I could live with - out love

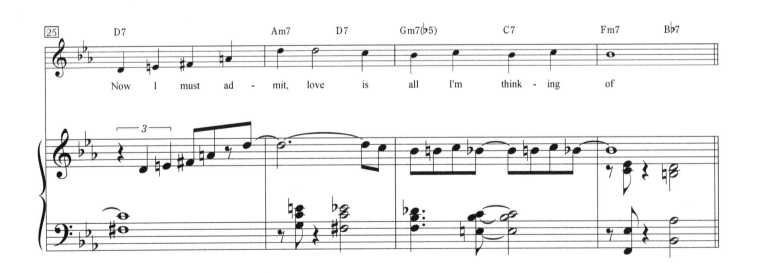

Now I must ad - mit, love is all I'm think - ing of

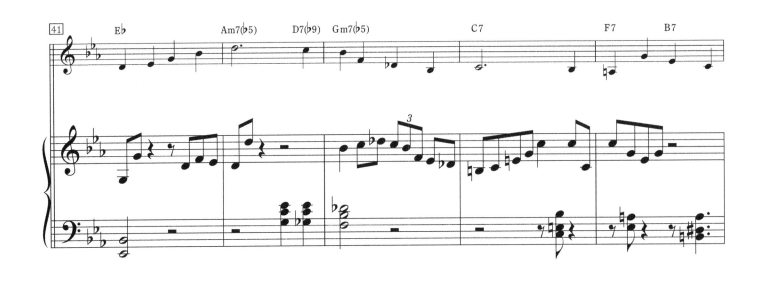

TAKE THE "A" TRAIN

writer: Billy Strayhorn

MMO 6009

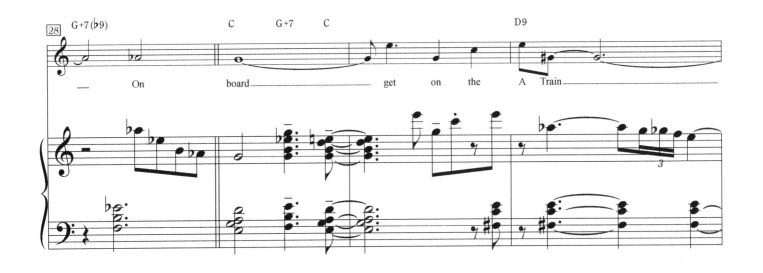

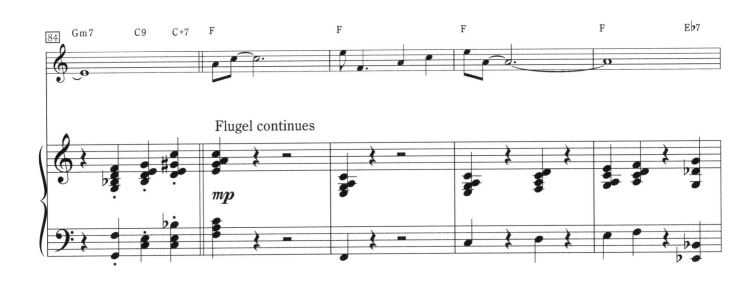

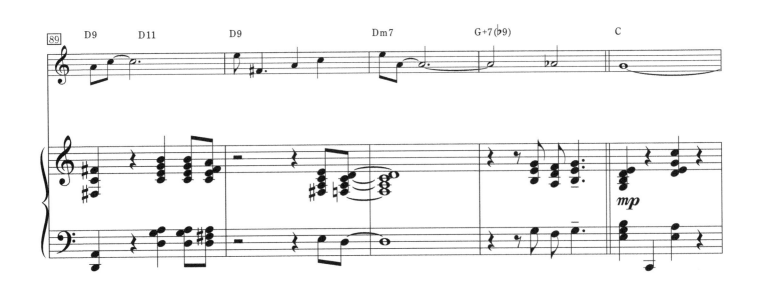

DARN THAT DREAM

Written by Eddie De Lange, Jimmy Van Heusen

MMO 6009

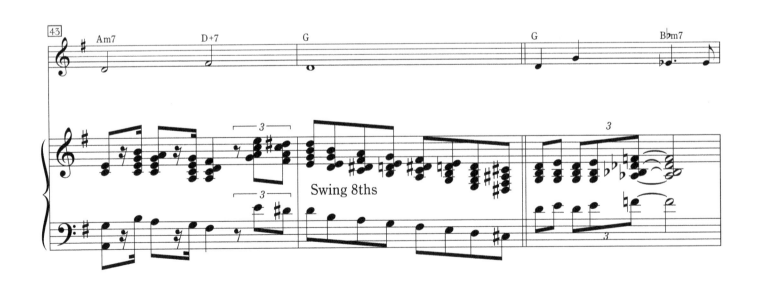

SOMEONE TO LIGHT UP MY LIFE

Written by De Moraes, Jobim, Lees

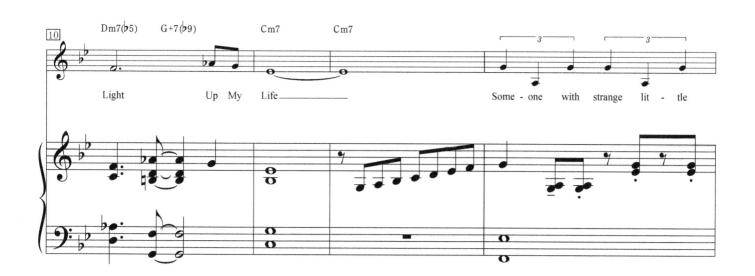

MMO 6009

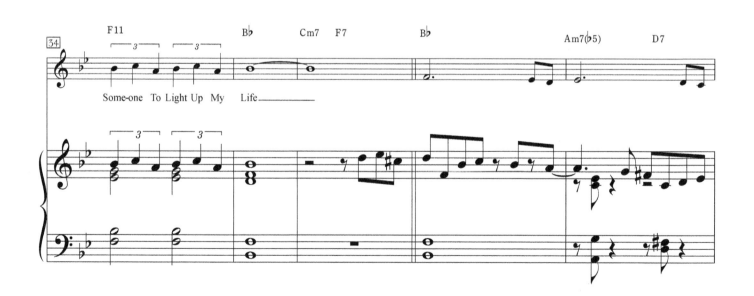

44

DREAM DANCING

by Cole Porter

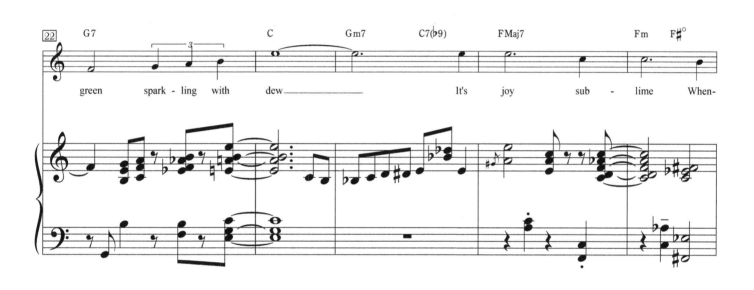

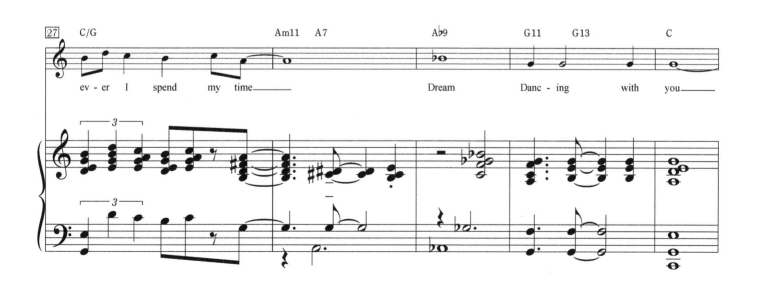

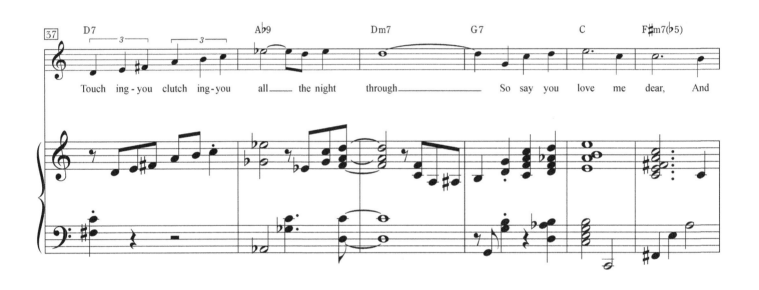

MORE THAN YOU KNOW

Written by Edward Eliscu, Billy Rose, Vincent Youmans

58

62

MMO 6009

SATIN DOLL

Written by Duke Ellington, Harry Mercer, Billy Strayhorn

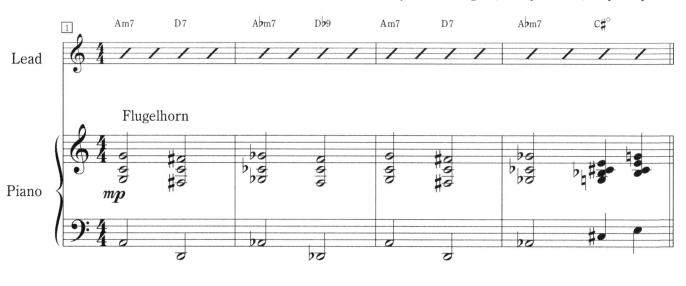

MMO 6009

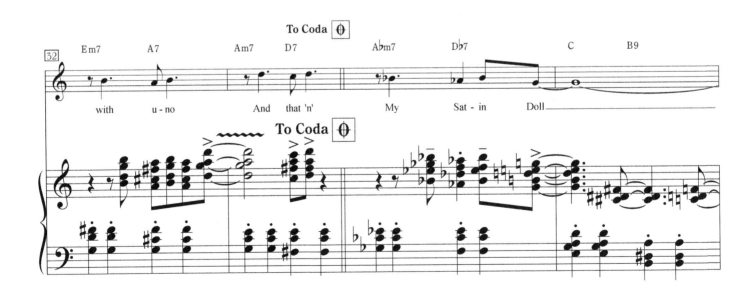

UNFORGETTABLE

Written by Mack Gordon

I HAD THE CRAZIEST DREAM

Written by Mack Gordon & Harry Warren

MMO 6009

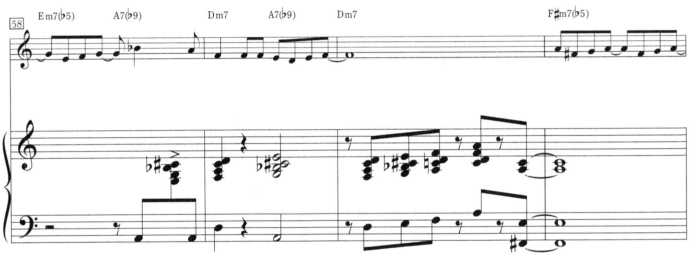

MORE GREAT JAZZ, BLUES & STANDARDS BOOKS FOR PIANO FROM

2 + 2 = 5 – A STUDY IN ODD TIMES
Accompaniment: Towson State College Jazz Ensemble
Conductor: Hank Levy
00400174 Book/CD Pack $14.99

20 DIXIELAND CLASSICS
Performed by Nat Pierce, piano
Accompaniment: The Dixieland All-Stars
00190506 Book/CD Pack $14.99

20 RHYTHM BACKGROUNDS
Performed by Dick Hyman & Nat Pierce, piano
Accompaniment: NBC Rhythm Section &
The All-Star Rhythm Section
00190523 Book/CD Pack $14.99

APRIL IN PARIS & OTHER FAVORITE LOVE SONGS
Performed by Jim Odrich, piano
00400797 Book/CD Pack $19.99

BACHARACH REVISITED
The Music of Burt Bacharach & Hal David
Performed by Jim Odrich, piano
00400668 Book/CD Pack $14.99

BLUES FUSION
Performed by Eric Kriss, piano & electric piano
00400226 Book/CD Pack $14.99

THE CONDON GANG – THE CHICAGO AND NEW YORK JAZZ SCENE
Performed by Ray Skjelbred, piano
Accompaniment: Hal Smith's Rhytmmakers
00400762 Book/2-CD Pack $14.99

FUNKDAWGS DON'T BITE – JAZZ FUSION UNLEASHED
Performed by Kyle Whitlock, keyboards
Accompaniment: Funkdawgs
00400167 Book/CD Pack $14.99

GEORGE GERSHWIN – RHAPSODY IN BLUE
Performed by Nayden Todorov, piano
Accompaniment: Plovdiv Philharmonic Orchestra
Conductor: Nayden Todorov
00400127 Book/Online Audio $24.99

THE ISLE OF ORLEANS
Performed by Tim Laughlin's New Orleans All-Stars
00400533 Book/2-CD Pack... $14.99

JAZZ FUSION – STUDIO SESSION BACKGROUNDS
Performed by Tom Collier, keyboards & percussion
Accompaniment: Howard Roberts, Guitar; Dan Dean, Electric Bass
00400186 Book/CD Pack $14.99

JAZZ PIANO TRIOS
Performed by Jim Odrich, piano
00400761 Book/Online Audio $19.99

THE JIM ODRICH EXPERIENCE
Performed by Jim Odrich, piano
00400707 Book/CD Pack $14.99

PLAY BALLADS WITH A BAND
Performed by Jim Odrich, piano
Accompaniment: The Bob Wilbur All-Star Band
00400670 Book/CD Pack $14.99

NEW ORLEANS CLASSICS
Performed by Tom McDermott, piano
Accompaniment: Tim Laughlin's New Orleans All-Stars
00400030 Book/CD Pack $19.99

SINATRA STANDARDS FOR PIANISTS
Performed by Jim Odrich, piano
00400709 Book/CD Pack $19.99

STRETCHIN' OUT WITH BLUES & STANDARDS
Performed by Tom Kohl, piano
Accompaniment: The Rhythm Masters
00400706 Book/CD Pack $14.99

SWING WITH A BAND
Performed by Jim Odrich, piano
00400671 Book/CD Pack $14.99

TAKE ONE
Accompaniment: Jersey State College Jazz Ensemble
Conductor: Dick Lowenthal
00400159 Book/CD Pack $14.99

To see a full listing of Music Minus One publications and
place your order from your favorite music retailer, visit
www.halleonard.com

HAL•LEONARD®

0920
320

Prices, contents, and availability subject to change without notice.